JAMAICA

By Sloane Gould and
Alicia Z. Klepeis

EXPLORING WORLD CULTURES

Cavendish Square

Published in 2024 by Cavendish Square Publishing, LLC
2544 Clinton Street, Buffalo, NY 14224

Second Edition

Website: cavendishsq.com

Library of Congress Cataloging-in-Publication Data

Names: Gould, Sloane, author. | Klepeis, Alicia, 1971- author.
Title: Jamaica / by Sloane Gould, Alicia Z. Klepeis.
Description: Second edition. | Buffalo, NY : Cavendish Square Publishing, [2024] | Series: Exploring world cultures | Includes index.
Identifiers: LCCN 2023011136 (print) | LCCN 2023011137 (ebook) | ISBN 9781502667649 (library binding) | ISBN 9781502667632 (paperback) | ISBN 9781502667656 (ebook)
Subjects: LCSH: Jamaica--Juvenile literature.
Classification: LCC F1872.2 .G68 2024 (print) | LCC F1872.2 (ebook) | DDC 972.92--dc23/eng/20230308
LC record available at https://lccn.loc.gov/2023011136
LC ebook record available at https://lccn.loc.gov/2023011137

Writers: Alicia Z. Klepeis; Sloane Gould (second edition)
Editor: Caitie McAneney
Copyeditor: Shannon Harts
Designer: Andrea Davison-Bartolotta

The photographs in this book are used by permission and through the courtesy of: Cover 5D Media/Shutterstock.com; p. 4 Sander Yoho/Shutterstock.com; p. 5 hyotographics/Shutterstock.com; p. 6 mmuenzl/Shutterstock.com; pp. 7, 19, 25 Photo Spirit/Shutterstock.com; p. 8 File:Duperly (1833) Destruction of the Roehampton Estate January 1832.png/Wikimedia Commons; p. 9 Debbie Ann Powell/Shutterstock.com; p. 10 Creative Photo Corner/Shutterstock.com; p. 11 File:Portia Miller Shoot.Jpeg/Wikimedia Commons; p. 13 (top) Pearl-diver/Shutterstock.com; p. 13 (bottom) Lucky-photographer/Shutterstock.com; p. 14 Thierry Eidenweil/Shutterstock.com; p. 15 Damsea/Shutterstock.com; pp. 16, 18, 22 Bussweh/Shutterstock.com; pp. 17, 23 Danita Delimont/Shutterstock.com; p. 20 Dwayne Chris/Shutterstock.com; p. 21 Andi de Boer/Shutterstock.com; p. 24 Andrew Park/Shutterstock.com; p. 26 Iurii Osadchi/Shutterstock.com; p. 27 Ververidis Vasilis/Shutterstock.com; p. 28 dapperland/Shutterstock.com; p. 29 Paul_Brighton/Shutterstock.com.

CPSIA compliance information: Batch #CS24CSQ: For further information contact Cavendish Square Publishing LLC at 1-877-980-4450.

Printed in the United States of America

CONTENTS

INTRODUCTION

Jamaica is known around the world for its beautiful environment, or natural surroundings. It's the third largest island in the Caribbean Sea. Its mountains, waterfalls, and beaches make it a top spot for travelers. Beautiful butterflies, birds, and plants are found in this **tropical** nation. It's an important **habitat** for many interesting animals, plants, and bugs, such as the huge Jamaican giant swallowtail butterfly.

The streamertail hummingbird, or "doctor bird," is the national bird of Jamaica.

Though different groups have ruled this island, Jamaica is a free country today. Jamaica has a rich culture, or way of life. It has been shaped by its history, landscape, and **traditions**. Much of the population has African roots because of a history of slavery there.

Unique, or special, arts, music, and writings come from this country. It's the birthplace of reggae music, which is enjoyed by people all over the world. Let's explore this exciting island nation!

Jamaica is in the Caribbean Sea, which is a sea of the Atlantic Ocean.

GEOGRAPHY

Jamaica is considered part of North America. The country covers an area of 4,411 square miles (11,424 square kilometers), divided into 14 parts called parishes. Because it's an island, it doesn't border any other countries. However, it's in the same area as Cuba and Haiti.

The Blue Mountains are in the eastern part of Jamaica. The central highland area has caves, waterfalls, sinkholes, and underground streams.

FACT!

Jamaica is a little smaller than the state of Connecticut.

People visit Montego Bay in Jamaica.

Some people visit sinkholes in Jamaica to swim in the clear blue water.

Jamaica has coastal lowlands in the north and south. These areas have beaches and farms. Jamaica has many rivers, including the Black River and the Rio Minho.

Jamaica has a hot and wet **climate** all year round. However, it is cooler in the mountains. This climate is perfect for many different plants, including ferns and orchids.

SINKHOLES

Sinkholes are large holes in the ground where water collects, wearing away underground rock. This can cause the ground to cave in.

HISTORY

Many believe that the Arawak were some of the first people to live in Jamaica. They're also called Taino. They came to Jamaica from South America around 600 CE. The Arawak called this island Xaymaca, meaning "land of wood and water."

FACT!
Slavery was outlawed in Jamaica in the 1830s.

Jamaica had many uprisings among its population of enslaved people.

In 1494, explorer Christopher Columbus landed in Jamaica and fought the Arawak for control. The Spanish ruled Jamaica until the English took control in 1655. In 1692, an earthquake destroyed the city of Port Royal. Survivors of the earthquake founded the city of Kingston.

Many enslaved people were brought from Africa to work on Jamaica's sugar plantations. Jamaica remained an English colony until 1962. Alexander Bustamante was Jamaica's first prime minister after Jamaica gained independence.

Many roads, schools, and hospitals were built during Bustamante's time in office.

ARAWAK INJUSTICE

Columbus and his men enslaved the Arawak people. Many Arawak died from being overworked and from diseases, or illnesses.

GOVERNMENT

Although Jamaica gained full independence in 1962, the king or queen of England is still called its chief of state. However, the country has its own constitution, or set of laws, and is self-governing. The capital of Jamaica is Kingston.

FACT!

The British monarch, or ruler, **appoints** a Jamaican governor-general who has been suggested by the Jamaican prime minister.

Jamaica's flag is black, yellow, and green.

Jamaica's government has three parts. The legislative, or lawmaking, part is parliament. Jamaica's parliament is made up of two houses. Its Senate has 21 members. Its House of Representatives has 63 members. They gather in the George William Gordon House to pass laws.

The executive part includes the ruler of England and prime minister of Jamaica. The courts make up the judicial part. They follow the country's constitution.

Portia Simpson Miller became the first female prime minister of Jamaica in 2006.

POLITICAL PARTIES

Jamaica has two main **political parties**—the Jamaica Labour Party and the People's National Party. Citizens can vote for who they want to speak for them in government.

THE ECONOMY

Jamaica has many goods and services that make up its economy, or its system of how money is made and used. Jamaica's most important trading partners include the United States, Canada, and China. Tourism, or people visiting Jamaica, is also a large part of its economy.

As a nation surrounded by water, Jamaica's fishers gather food from the sea, both to eat and to sell. In the countryside, farmers grow many crops such as sugarcane, bananas, and yams. Jamaican workers make many different products. These range from everyday items like clothing and paper to drinks such as rum and coffee. Jamaican Blue Mountain coffee is enjoyed around the world for its special taste.

SERVICE JOBS

About two out of three Jamaican workers have service jobs. Some work in schools, restaurants, and resorts.

Jamaica's currency is the Jamaican dollar.

Jamaican resorts offer beautiful water views.

FACT!

A resort is a place people go to have fun on vacation.

THE ENVIRONMENT

Jamaica's beautiful tropical environment is one reason many people visit. Many plants and animals call this land home. However, Jamaica's people, plants, and animals need clean air and water to live. Water pollution is a problem in Jamaica. Oil spills and **industrial** waste threaten the water quality here. Pollution can harm the coral reefs along Jamaica's coast.

FACT!

Overfishing and storms harm coral reefs and surrounding water habitats.

Iguanas, crocodiles, and manatees are rare today in Jamaica because of habitat loss and hunting.

Air pollution is also a problem in parts of Jamaica. Sometimes, there is smog, or fog mixed with smoke or air pollution. The two main sources of this pollution are cars and industrial activities.

Jamaica is working to get more of its electricity from clean sources. One example of a clean energy source is solar power, or power from the sun.

TREES

Much of Jamaica's original forests have been cut down. People cut trees down mainly for agriculture but also for new buildings and resorts.

Coral reefs are structures formed by the skeletons of small animals called coral.

THE PEOPLE TODAY

People in Jamaica come from many different backgrounds and cultures. More than 90 percent of Jamaicans have African roots. The **ancestors** of many Black Jamaicans came from West Africa.

FACT!
About 2.8 million people live in Jamaica.

The biggest city in Jamaica is Kingston, home to around 937,000 people.

Around 3 percent of Jamaica's people have Indian roots. Many of their ancestors came to Jamaica from India for work. Jamaica is also home to several smaller groups of people. The country has communities of German, Chinese, and Middle Eastern people. All of these groups brought their own cultures and traditions to Jamaica. The country's national motto is "Out of Many, One People."

IRISH IN JAMAICA

There's a large population of people with Irish roots in Jamaica. British people brought Irish people to Jamaica in the 1600s as workers. Some were enslaved.

Girls dance outside their school in Kingston.

LIFESTYLE

About 57 percent of people in Jamaica live an urban lifestyle. That means they live in cities or towns. Some live in apartments. Others live in houses. Families here often have cell phones and televisions.

Crime is a big problem in some neighborhoods. Kingston has some areas where housing conditions are poor.

People in the city might walk, ride a bike, or take a bus to work.

Other Jamaicans live a rural lifestyle. That means they live in the countryside. The pace of life is often slower here. Jamaicans in rural areas may work as miners. Some have jobs at resorts or in national parks. Some grow crops to sell or feed their families. Some are fishers, especially those who live on the water.

WOMEN IN JAMAICA

Many Jamaican women today have jobs outside of the home. They work as businesspeople, lawyers, and engineers.

FACT!

In Jamaica, it's common for children, parents, and grandparents to live together.

Around 20,000 Jamaicans work in fishing.

RELIGION

Many different religions, or faiths, are practiced in Jamaica. The constitution grants freedom of religion, which means people can believe in any faith. Religion is important to many Jamaican people. Around two out of three people here are Christian, specifically Protestant. There are also smaller groups of Christians that include Roman Catholics and Jehovah's Witnesses.

FACT!
Jamaica has no official religion.

This large Christian (Methodist) church is in Kingston.

In addition to Christians, Jamaica is also home to small Hindu and Buddhist populations. There are also Muslims. Jamaica's Jewish community has a long history. More than 21 percent of Jamaica's people do not follow any religion at all.

A small percent of Jamaicans follow a religion called Rastafari. They believe Haile Selassie I (originally called Ras Tafari), who became emperor of Ethiopia in 1930, was God. They follow rules about food and do not cut their hair.

This is a Rastafarian statue.

CHRISTIAN CELEBRATIONS

Christian church services are held every Sunday in cities and villages throughout Jamaica. Christian holidays, such as Christmas and Easter, are celebrated.

LANGUAGE

Most people speak English in Jamaica. The country's government uses English. People speak English for business matters. In school, children are also taught in English.

Jamaican English sounds different from the English people speak in the United States. Most Jamaicans speak Jamaican patois (PA-twa). Patois is the dialect spoken by a particular group.

FACT!
A dialect is a form of a language that is spoken in a specific place or by a specific group of people.

English is the official language of Jamaica, so most signs are in English.

Jamaican patois is a local dialect developed as enslaved Africans in Jamaica spoke with their English-speaking enslavers. Jamaican patois has its own vocabulary and grammar. For example, instead of "What's up?" they would say, "Wah gwaan?"

In 2016, a woman from England created a doll named Toya that speaks Jamaican patois. The doll has become a popular item around the world. It helps people learn about and **appreciate** Jamaican language and culture.

OTHER LANGUAGES

Immigrants who have come to Jamaica from different places may speak languages other than English. Chinese is just one example.

Schools may teach Spanish and French in addition to English.

ARTS AND FESTIVALS

Bright colors are common in Jamaica, and they can be seen in the island's artwork. Artists liven up even the nation's poorest neighborhoods by making colorful **murals**. Things Jamaicans make and sell—such a bags, clothing, and jewelry—are often in bright colors.

FACT!

Paintings and carvings made by the Taino people are the island's earliest artworks.

These Jamaican dancers perform a traditional dance.

Dance is another important part of Jamaican culture. The mento is a traditional dance performed here, but mento also refers to a type of Jamaican folk music. It features instruments called bongo drums and the rhumba box. Around the world, Jamaica is known for reggae music.

Jamaica has festivals throughout the year. Reggae Sumfest celebrates reggae music every summer. The Jamaican Carnival, usually in April, celebrates Jamaican culture with special foods, music, dancing, and colorful costumes.

INDEPENDENCE DAY

Jamaicans celebrate Independence Day on August 6. This is the day of their independence from the United Kingdom. They celebrate with big parades.

People visit the Bob Marley Museum in Kingston to celebrate this famous reggae musician.

FUN AND PLAY

With tropical weather all year round, Jamaica provides many opportunities to be active. In their free time, many Jamaicans enjoy spending time at the beach. People often swim and fish. Water activities like scuba diving and snorkeling are also popular with local people and tourists visiting Jamaica.

Despite being a tropical island, Jamaica has a bobsled team in the Winter Olympics.

Lots of Jamaican people enjoy sports. Soccer is a popular sport here. Many people also play cricket. Basketball and track and field are also popular in Jamaica.

Usain Bolt is a famous athlete from Jamaica. He is their biggest track and field star. He has won Olympic gold medals for his sprinting, or running quickly for a short distance.

FACT!

Usain Bolt set the world record for both the 100-meter and 200-meter sprints.

Usain Bolt is famous around the world.

CRICKET

Cricket is similar to baseball. It is played with a bat and ball. Cricket was created in England and spread to its **colonies** over time.

FOOD

Jamaican food is loved by people around the world. One of the most popular parts of Jamaican **cuisine** is jerk meat. Jerk refers to the spices used to season meat as well as the way it is smoked and grilled. Jerk can be traced back hundreds of years to the ways formerly enslaved people and Native people cooked meat in mountain areas.

FACT!
The country's national dish is ackee (a native fruit) and saltfish.

Jerk chicken is a popular food in Jamaica.

Because Jamaica is surrounded by water, seafood is common. As a tropical island, Jamaica offers many different fruits, such as bananas, pineapples, and papayas. Juice, coffee, and rum are popular drinks here. Like the island itself, Jamaican food is full of color and rich with tradition.

RASTAFARIAN CUISINE

Rastafarians mostly eat fruits and vegetables, and other things that come from the earth. They do not eat meat.

Jamaicans make patties shaped like half-moons stuffed with meat.

GLOSSARY

ancestor: A family members from whom a person has descended.

appoint: To choose for a position.

appreciate: To accept the worth or value of something.

climate: The average weather conditions of a place over a period of time.

colony: A piece of land under the control of another country.

cuisine: A style of cooking.

habitat: The natural home for plants, animals, and other living things.

industrial: Having to do with making things.

mural: A large picture painted onto a wall.

political party: A group whose members hold the same general beliefs about how government should work.

tradition: A way of thinking, behaving, or doing something that's been used by people in a particular society for a long time; traditional means having to do with the ways of doing things in a culture that are passed down from parents to children.

tropical: Having to do with the warm parts of Earth.

FIND OUT MORE

Books

Levit, Joe. *Track and Field's G.O.A.T.: Usain Bolt, Jackie Joyner-Kersee, and More*. Minneapolis, MN: Lerner Publishing Group, 2021.

Mather, Charis. *A Visit to Jamaica*. Minneapolis, MN: Bearport Publishing, 2023.

Website

Jamaica
kids.nationalgeographic.com/geography/countries/article/jamaica
Explore this exciting Caribbean country with *National Geographic Kids*!

Video

My Country Jamaica
www.youtube.com/watch?v=ZzooHlq8ZWs
Learn more about Jamaican people with this tribute video to a Jewish Jamaican woman.

Publisher's note to educators and parents: Our editors have carefully reviewed these websites to ensure that they are suitable for students. Many websites change frequently, however, and we cannot guarantee that a site's future contents will continue to meet our high standards of quality and educational value. Be advised that students should be closely supervised whenever they access the internet.

INDEX